House of Deer

Sasha Steensen

House of Deer

Sasha Steensen

FENCE BOOKS

Albany, New York

cover photo courtesy of the author and her mother

Cover and book design by Rebecca Wolff

Published in the United States by Fence Books, Science Library, 320
University at Albany, 1400 Washington Avenue, Albany, NY 12222

www.fenceportal.org

Fence Books are printed in Canada by The Prolific Group and distributed
by Small Press Distribution and Consortium Book Sales and Distribution.

Library of Congress Cataloguing in Publication Data
Steensen, Sasha [1963-]
House of Deer/Sasha Steensen

Library of Congress Control Number: 2014932376

ISBN 13: 978-1-934200-67-4

FIRST EDITION
10 9 8 7 6 5 4 3 2

Fence Books are published in partnership with the University at Albany
and the New York State Writers Institute, and with help from the New
York State Council on the Arts and the National Endowment for the Arts.

Grateful acknowledgment is made to the editors of the following
publications in which some of these poems first appeared: *The Offending
Adam, Ink Node, Word/for Word, Bombay Gin, Similar Peaks, Thuggery and Grace,
Zing Magazine, Black Warrior Review, Academy of American Poets Daily Poetry
Series, 751 Magazine, Octopus Magazine*, and *Free Verse*. Thank you to Sommer
Browning and Tony Mancus of Flying Guillotine Press for publishing the
chapbook, *A History of the Human Family*. This book owes a great debt to the
following individuals, each of whom served as readers and/or counselors on
all things family: Dan and Kristy Beachy-Quick, Matthew Cooperman, Aby
Kaupang, Becky Robinson, Jennifer Johnson, and Rebecca Wolff. Mostly,
thank you to my families, Gordon, Phoebe, and Greta Hadfield, and
especially Rob, Gretchen, and Erik Steensen.

FOR MY FAMILIES

As to the name of Deer . . . The spelling of the word has varied at different times. In its first form it is Déar, 'tear' in harmony with the traditional belief of its origin. In the Charter of David I, it is Dér. It afterwards appears as Deir, Dere, and Deer. The last has been the ordinary spelling for a long time, and I have retained . . . in the belief that, as the word is commonly pronounced, this is . . . nearest . . . earliest.

JOHN STUART, *The Book of Deer*

In this in which the wild deer
Startle, and stare out.

GEORGE OPPEN, "Psalm"

Table of Contents

Domestication and the Chase

we took shelter from where
                why

                        the forest feels its way forward and lives
                        lives seemingly forever

                        lives lives that are all ours

hey, Lantern, you cannot keep to yourself
in such dark night
things you wish to hide

                why
                I can't say

we went darker into what was not there
& found a fawn

deeper inside her mother

she was so young and tender
the bones as well as the flesh

& yet we thought
 it was very good
& yet we thought
 had it been born
it would have entered
 and walked
& yet we thought

not   it behooves me to speak

we set out across the field in light snow
afire with meat

       our dogs treed

 what they could not find

we finally see, like Antigone,
shame is not something to wear behind one's ear

rather, like all god's blessings
it enters through the eyes

to be a sister is to sing while burying
to sing of the tree

of the creek
& of the antlered thoughts descending there to drink

to speak we
cross the lake
we look across the lake
we see in its depths of lake

what exactly
do we see

but why
did I not spot you
brother capsized
who taught me to swim

right then

what beautiful words buoy up but

a mortal ripens like corn
and like corn is born
again

if ever I were to return
I would tell of the pearl
well guarded
in the belly of her mother

I would tell the world
an ingenious hunter
skins his prey
& slits the hide

if ever I were to return
an ingenious hunter
conceals himself
by stepping inside

My Trees Knot Up and a Forest Make

how does one become the mother of the man who will be
the father of her children but by gratified desire but that
is simply a description of addiction what's the difference
between habit and that but if there is one its joys dark
and translucent let us sense a heaven hell he'll speak to us
of weakness either way to fill you're the poppy of a bundle
of poppies you must know heroin is the desire of desire
I will not think of this hard home as land to come back
to but I will say you fed me everything that moveth shall
be meat for thee I have always said I could not will not
bring forth but more than that your hands and all they
taught me how to do the electricity created by bringing
them together in enthusiasm enthusiastic prayer in prayer
one hand knows the other knows what the other does as
if it were its brother rather its sister its mother pushed
together with sufficient pressure a hand stilled sees its
own way forward sees that way madness lies in its own
piss-filled bathwater magnificent and straightway I don't
mean to be always here looking whithersoever actually I
like to look upward and see what way is all open all sky all
the way to the smallest opening of light but the hole digs
itself deeper have you seen her open hardened heart lay
itself down for you in the thousands of ways she did do
will do a million times over give ye them to eat the loaves
the loaves are plenty prepare then the other way that way
blindness lies we do not know if the meat in your pocket
will rot or will we find food everlasting still understanding
of course that we shall be like a handful of people roaming
for months some house room to room thinking we were
lost but you knew the hall the ventricle so well a still place
within you but did you know half of all parents don't kiss
their young children on the lips too intimate what sort
of still distance is left between them and the asses they
wipe thousands of times what do they hope to maintain
but themselves as themselves comforting themselves with

a life created committed back to the body abundantly from which it came a buck stilled like The Deer Hunter's one shot one shot is beauty you remember the trees why can't we just go back there because a prophet is not without honor save in his own country in his own home and we had to grow something new something like Nicky in some dirty steelmill town drunk on the train tracks the night before Vietnam "I like the way the trees are in the mountains, all the different ways the trees are too" the trees under which this wound heals over still still visible still

Family

If family is a body, learn its anatomy:
It has the head of a house.
Each room is a cortex of the brain.
Contrary to popular illustration, the windows are not eyes,
      but teeth.
It is impossible to tell whether a house is smiling or frowning.
Are the members of its body subterranean, perhaps the roots
      of nearby trees?
Or, are its extremities hung for the neighbors to see, the head
      shaded heartily above?

It hears its own head, sorting these parts out.
"Doom is the House without / the Door—"

There have been some makeshift additions.
In the basement, among the mold, discarded toys, musical
      instruments, and Christmas decorations, its heart beats
            solemnly on.
A deep freeze sits nearby holding pounds of meat, frozen
      vegetables from the harvest, bones for the dog, and other
            miscellany.
A ribcage. A ribcage. A ribcage.
The deck overlooking the property provides an aerial view
      of all that is outside, of all the foreign bodies that enter
            with each breath.
The house, heated by wood-burning stoves, has an invisible
      respiratory system.
Each time a member leaves, it takes a body out into the world
      and brings back a body to enter the family.

When you are outside looking in, you see windows lit in
      estranged light.
When you are inside looking out, you see worlds lit in strange
      light.

8

The family bought a rural plot & planted a garden.

The family formed thoughts.

Within these thoughts, eggs hatched, animals were born, little
wars formed.   Each thought said unspeakable things to
the other thoughts.

As you know, unspoken thoughts rot.

The family had a creek running through their plot.

The family liked watching the bobwhites dive down for their
dinner.

How inconsiderate of time to throw light upon these thoughts.

Longtime residents of the nearby farms watched.

In the 70s more than a million hippies went back to
the land.

Somehow, they fit in.

Perhaps it was the yardful of cars.

The family loved its overgrown plot.

The family loved its dilapidated barn.

The family would have loved its Amish neighbors,

would have loved their handmade furniture

free-of-particle-board,

were it not for the unspeakable rift

—rows of empty seats on the bus—

 that kept them apart.

The family loved its silo where so many cats drowned.

The family even loved the bats in her belfry.

Until they burned it down.

It was their bicentennial.

It was where they learned to ride a bicycle.

It was their scarf of earth.

It was surrounded by hills.

Like nothing else in Ohio,

it was where they placed their pails

of bird & bush & dying fish.

House of Deer

'Tis I can delve and plough, love
And you can spin and sew;
And we'll settle on the banks of
The pleasant O-hi-o

THE EARLY SONGS OF UNCLE SAM

Little Deerfamily Near

were all things madein
the house on Hopkins Road
or were all things
madeout

it's like 70s ruralamerica
so many things
you recognize

your own eyes

and minehouse
its deerness hanging out

pulltab tops
parties in our yard
andthennot
it'sland we come back to
andthennot

father hadhad
his share
and now asleep on the chair

like
exceptionalclearness
like hart
like
birdtotheark

like metallic wallpaper
&the Dirty War
like microwavesandbeta
like Hee Haw
like pinball

like1976
snow & dirtroad no one drives down
but us &other neighborfolk
&nowhere to go
but backtotheland
&Hopkins Road
seems a good place to try something new
but so will 1982

if it weren't for the garden
&the yard
&the live oaks
&the hearth bolted to the land
&&

like even-toed ungulates
like ruminants &their relatives
like seahippos
like landwhales
sound of deer changing direction &then turning back

1977& we came too
for summer parties
&midnight
in the basement
mounds of children
in mounds of sleepingbags
&clump of elders in the yard
&truth be told I wasn't sleeping
&truth be told
I never heard of keyparties
till recently
we lived so farout
tents dot the farm

On Birth

1974Chagrin Falls, Ohio
just moments before
he ushers ininfancy
Drunk &Wondrous as chipped twigs
he walks through a glass door

we lived on the brink of a gorge
that was flat all around

like moon landings
&burdens
&massacres in

Munich skin of the book
skin of the deer

like many-yeared
like landward
like me now groping
around
like skin of the buck

                    a great depth of moss

like the hole that begins this story
like the spring the gophers dug dug
or the summer the old keys long &rusty
wrenched their way up?

or was it hunting season
heap of bluets
heap of hart
heap
heap
heap of
        indian summer
heat of

1978I found them newborn
&whimpering in the tall grass
I had to cleanopen
their eyes
to the world
I had to seethemsee
the ditch daisies & oleanders
the hosannas
the woodlands & greenleaves
they had to know
the thawedcreek
the gnarly nest
experience&expressionmake
nothing's safe
where children's tenderest wishes leap

2009Between   gathering   &   giving
I write *lurch*

one word &then
they need something again

I never knew howungrateful howhungry howcold howangry
howsleepless
children canbe

I screamwhisper

Out House
ourhouse
shape of the body we eat

1804woodsmen &woodswomen &woodschildren
cut a road right before you
&hereinafter
ahistory of Garrettsville, Ohio:
like gristmill &woolenmill &sawmill
like carriage factory &chair factory &pail factory
like factory of linseedoil
like distillery &tannery &foundry
&largest maple center in the world
like home of Hart &home of Crane
like deereye near as large as an elephant's
but allblack withoutwhite
except she looketh back

like Camp
David
The Native
Ornament
the Dream
of going Back
to the Land&

the neighbors gunned an animal
his heart roasted and snaking on a skewer

like Dallas Dillon's pet raccoons
&his cats, Cheech and Chong
identity=themakeofyourcar
like The Dukes of Hazzard
like decapitating snakes
like sledding behind snowmobiles
&setting the forest onfire
like somemustang=fastest girl around

like something between town and own
likedrunkdrunk
&nothing to do but drive

we owe our lives to him who gave them
that we always made it home

like the Amish on the nextfarm
its just oneversion of onefamily
but it's ours

like drunkand
all those aroundhim

like town ofhicks
like town ofrifles
like pre-winters
with freezer
fullofcoon

like venison
&family cohesion

he finally came around
&for good

he &his wagon
&our autumn hayrides
he and his hitch
&now he never falls off

garden like lava like lamp
like goodbye vietnam&

like Christine Chubbuck
like Hudson, Ohio
anchored to the land&
woundeth on tv

before the freeze
before the shock

we made porridge
we made messofwheat

&like
a surface
every day
lichens&
she fills
for winter
on
the houses
how many
this year
who
looking
hides
up
the beads
his deerness
we must say
what violence
I want
who comes
like a curlew

logging
of the forest
there lies
loaded
her trunk
we have
all five sides
to our
owls
in the
uproots
ahead lurking
skinned
to dry
of blood
to me
our
is lodged
for our
forth stepping
with its

in 1979
mulched
avery
with ferns
with firewood
elbowroom
until here come
countryside
hung themselves
forest
but a husband
be
and hung
but for
wiped up
until
goodbyes
in the name
daughter: Violet
softly into the water
swarm

of lightning bugs but us little deerfamily precious yokefellows
nigh in the skirt of the woods

Election Day

There's more on the periphery, but the blackest edges
    encroach, like a photo on fire—
what we now know about small town life in rural Ohio
    growing sharper.

I will try to tell you about my childhood hill so that you
might see it for yourself. Behind it, there is a once-red-
now-dilapidated barn leaning to the right with various
rusty garden tools strewn about its floor, and hay stacked
on its half-caved in second story. At its bottom is a
winding creek. To the right, and itself slightly sloped,
there's a garden, and to the left, just where it flattens out,
a white house, a 150-year old Greek Revival with gables
facing the street. I still have told you nothing of the hill
    itself, but what is there to say?
It is grassy and then it is snowy and then it is grassy again.

I've always had an eye for seeing without knowing what
    the other eye is for.
Janet and Burt are there in the distance, cleaning their
    shotguns or sweeping the steps,
and depending on which eye I see through, the neighbors
look like trees, and the trees like neighbors gathering
around the mind's property line from which I bring forth
the hill, or rather, the barn and all that surrounds it.

What will appear to us next cannot quite enter the story.
There are textures of every place that have yet to change:
Mullets and feathered hair; The Skylane Drive-Thru
Liquor store; Muscle cars—GTOs; Roadrunners;
Cameros, raccoon tails dangling from their antennas and
graduation tassels from their rearview mirrors; Classic
Rock; the strawberry social and the soapbox derby;
Roachclips with feathers; Half a cow from Freezer Beef;
Dunebuggies; Snowmobiles; and Four-Wheelers; Gee-

Ville Auto Parts; decapitated snakes and squirrel hunting;
39 cent Sundays; The Brick with its burgers and pinball
machines; shot-up stop signs; marijuana planted sideways
in the forest so it can't be seen from the air.

It's not just a form of episodic memory in which
        boundaries between then and now are
smoothed over so that a coherent narrative of a
        permanent self with a personal past emerges.
The town has barely changed.
There are, no doubt, principles of plot construction
grounding our ordinary memories. We trace a line,
sometimes broken, sometimes fused, through all narratives,
a route finally continuous with the present
        location of the remembering "I."

This memory, like a cuckoo clock controlled by its carefully
balanced mechanism, comes right out of its house:
I go to the church on the town's circle with my mother.
I wait in one of the three lines forming in the front of the
        three booths with maroon curtains.
After the sounds of old levers shifting and curtain rings
traveling over metal rods, out come the triumphant adults,
some with children, some without, and I think, whatever it
is that goes on inside is something I am not
        meant to see others do.
But one's own mother is, for many years, the single
        exception.
Once inside, I discover I am too short to see the polling
machine, but I can see other feet to the right and left,
and we are inside a few minutes, and then we file out, and
others file in, and we wrap ourselves in scarves and hats
and leave the church, traveling around the circle, returning
to our warm home.

That memory, an ember on a pile of dead leaves, makes
    one-third of my mind think:
Buckeye state, I've only so much readiness to come home today
and on my path, the pointy nipples of acorns underfoot pierce my
    shoe's sole.
And what about the other two-thirds of my mind?
I've defended you.

This is the sound of middling minds banging together:
growing up, we were told we were mid-westerners, middle-
people, middle-minded, middle-centered, middle-aged,
middle-class, middle-men, middle-of-the-road.
We were told the middle is where one wants to be, the
    heart and the heartland right in the middle.
In middle school, geography and biology were the same
    class.
On the map, we were just to the right of the middle, near
    the top of the body without a head, Lake Erie lapping
    tenderly at our neck.
When we crossed the hall to the next classroom and
    looked up at the laminated, fleshless
        body unrolled before us, we found the heart,
            hanging just to the right of the middle,
the Superior Vena Cava leading upward not unlike the
    Ohio-Erie Canal.
But what if the middle spreads, the middles seeps, the
    middle sounds to its edges?
What happens if the middle-ground, which is often the
    low-ground, is believed to be the high-ground?
The heart can be treated so that we live longer with a
    sicker and sicker heart, forever meddling with the rest
        of the body's functions.

But it doesn't serve me to worry.
Instead it needles me.
I was taught:

Have your latchstrings always out, meaning, be hospitable.
But I cannot.
I would have let you in if you had just knocked,
but I've spent all the time I have.
There are children to clothe and dishes to do, and it's just not
    the kind of poem where everything belongs.

Fragments
after Hopkins

The sun just risen
flares his wet brilliance in the dintless heaven

Did I finish this morning's morning given
before mid-noon

its sickle-stink
brooding about until a fire flames forth

from the cross-tree I spot a darkling willow
the sun deadened

evening's evening
a dent in timber, then smoldering embers

I caught this night
Night's water, now pay fast attention, heaven

what happened happened, I speared a fish straight thru
its gilly heart

I'm not sorry
narrowness surrounds me vast, moving faster

O after noon begging me to be quiet
with my bucket

tied to my side
fishingpole whacking at flies and besides the fish

is multiple and warring with each other
as a fire

in the canoe
good for roasting dwindles with the day, hurray!

Bring in the fog, then, and mope around the house
Blame God then and

mope around the yard
But watch out, the world is charged with the grandeur

of God, Oh I

know Ohio
how squirrels on my roof sound like a stampede

and feed grows scarce with each passing hour our
gilly heart spared,

tackled, laid out
to dry in the sun, as on a hammock, but less fun

oh waterspout of wildfire turned off
leafmold growing

spawns small nesters
with all sorts of sicknesses chased away pale

or dimly ticks
call neighbors over to peer upon our pocks

how stuttery your sprung is as if you can
not speak to God

sores in the mouth
sprung hotly so that chicken tastes like pigeon

who has my hat
but the little life giggling in the corner

she's so dear to me my daughter tho she fits
barely in the poem

but I force it
so that she might have a small place among you

damn sentimental
to hell or wanwood forest, whatever's quicker

as it may be
I ate, slept, and spit on Hopkins his silence

lights a mile of green grass ahead and all the darkness
     stays dark
as it should be

The family's relationship with itself was strained.

This was meant to be a story about Hart Crane.

This was meant to be a story about his name.

The imaginary horns on the forehead of a cuckold.

Bird, fern, deer, buckthorn, machine & truffle.

This was meant to be a story about Harold.

This was meant to be a story about his "birthplace," his
  "permanent home—"

his father's hotel in Chagrin Fall's, Garrettsville's 2.5 square
  miles.

This was meant to be a history of Ohio.

Main vein of the heartland, begetter of hogs,

your glistening sausages circle the globe.

My how you've grown!

This was meant to be a story of happenstance.

As Sherwood Anderson later learned, there really is a Winesburg.

The family traded its only car for a motorcycle.

This was meant to be a story of coincidence.

Crane's father, candymaker, invented the lifesaver.

The motorcycle rode along the outskirts of town,

past the mill, the roller rink, & Crane's Dad's house.

This was meant to be a story of euphemism.

Should you visit, be sure to find it.

Doubling as his Dad's tombstone,

Crane's memorial reads *Lost at Sea*.

This was meant to be a story, and it may be.

Learning to recognize a story is a long and difficult process.

It is the domain of the family,

meaning it begins in infancy.

Its importance is born of its difficulty.

Nursery Rhyme

The thorntree snags its bird by berries
like the word its thought

a little blood down the walk

until from the sky falls
a dictionary

on the little bird
and the berry

leaving
a lot of blood on the walk.

A swarm of bees
breaches the family

and warms us in winter
with its stings

until a word intercedes
to ask what word casts

what other word out

until the weathercock bade
us west

until the recollection
of collective memory

follows the members
of the—

& a bowl of sound
beyond the thorntree
bids come forth

bird on the walk
swarm of bees—
family.

The Girl & The Deer

THEN HIS DEER MOTHER TOLD HIM EVERYTHING
AND NOW
I will tell you everything
From here

> "The Boy and the Deer," *The Art of Zuni Storytelling*
> (Dennis Tedlock)

THE GIRL

This is a story the writer cannot tell. If she could tell it, she
would tell it plainly. If she could tell it, she would tell it swiftly,
as if singing. If she could tell it, she would tell it in their
language. The writer's neighbor, the daughter of a farmer, was
in the fields, checking the crops. She was always in the fields,
checking the crops. She spent all day in the fields, plucking
earworms from the feedcorn or searching the soybeans for
black leaf blight. It seems while she spent all her hours in
the fields, the Sun-Father had made her pregnant. This is the
foundation of the story she would tell if she could tell it. Her
belly grew large. Her belly grew large as she walked in the
fields for a time. Her belly grew large, very very large. Her
belly grew large and then the ache in her belly grew large.
When the ache in her belly grew large, she walked across the
field, across the street, through the writer's property and into
Eagle Creek Reserve. She followed the creek. She went on
until she came to the bog. She sat below a large oak tree on
the edge of the bog near the creek. The ache in her belly grew
large. The ache in her belly grew very very large. She could not
see for a moment, and the ache in her belly grew larger until
the little baby came out. When the little baby came out, she
dug a hole. In the hole, she made a bed of leaves and boggy
grass, and she placed the baby in the hole, atop the bed. She
washed herself and her clothes in the creek, and she followed
the creek back to the fields, and the fields back to her home.

This is another part of the story the writer can't tell. The deer who lived on the Eagle Creek Reserve were going to the creek to drink. And the little baby was crying. The little baby was born in need of tenderness. The writer thinks, this must be the basis of all stories. The twin fawns on their way to the creek with their mother heard the little baby crying. And when they came upon the crying, they walked in the direction of the hole with the bed of leaves and boggy grass. The deer mother resolved to take the baby from the hole, from its bed. She resolved to save the baby. The deer mother nursed and nursed the girl until she was satisfied, and the fawns slept near her, with their fur around her. And they lived this way for some time. The mother nursed and nursed, the fawns slept with their fur around her. Often the part of every story like this remains untold.

THE DEER

The girl and the deer lived on this way until winter
approached. When winter approached, the deer mother knew
that the girl, who had no fur, needed clothing. She was naked
and needed clothing. One night the deer mother left the
fawns nestled together. She followed the creek to the writer's
property. She crept through the writer's garden, through the
fields, past the houses and on to Nelson Ledges. She went
over three ledges and down into a village situated in a ravine.
This village, alive only at night, was the home of the deer's
ancestors. This is a story within a story the writer also cannot
tell because who would believe her? The ancestral spirits were
lavishly clothed, and as the deer mother told them of the story
of the girl, each one gave over an article of clothing. The spirit
whose face was bordered by a dark light gave a skirt of woven
hemp; the spirit whose hair was like the Milky Way gave a
shirt of cotton; the spirit whose ears where squash blossoms
gave a wool sweater; the spirit whose nose was like the ledge
under which he lived gave a pair of leather boots; The spirit
whose hands were tree limbs in winter gave a hat so tightly
woven a blade of grass could not have penetrated its threads.
The mother returned to her fawns. When the mother
returned to her fawns, she clothed her daughter. Often some
part of every story goes untold. The mother and the deer and
the girl lived on like this for some time.

THE GIRL

When spring arrived, the farmers complained to the
rangers that their fields were overrun with deer. The
rangers allowed the farmers to enter the Reserve for a
short time to hunt the deer who were overrunning their
fields. The girl's uncle entered the Reserve with his rifle,
and he walked quietly and slowly on a ridge overlooking
a valley. In the valley the uncle saw a herd of deer. On
the ridge the uncle raised his rifle. As he raised his rifle
to aim, he saw the girl running in circles around the deer.
If the writer were the uncle, she would tell the story like
this: I saw a girl running in circles around the deer. I
lowered my rifle back to my side. I paused for a moment
wondering how the girl came to live with the deer, and
I returned to my home. During dinner, I told the story
of the girl and the deer: "Today, while I was hunting in
the Reserve I walked upon a ridge overlooking a valley;
there was a herd of deer. There was a herd of deer, and
there was girl running in circles around the deer." When
the uncle told the story of the girl and the deer, the
entire family was confused and intrigued. The farmer's
daughter insisted they find out who the girl was. The
farmer's daughter insisted the brother go with his friends
the following morning to find out who the girl was, to
bring the girl to the farm to answer who she was, she who
played with the deer.

The Girl and the Deer

That night, the deer mother told the girl that her uncle would come looking for her, and that she must run and run, and then she must stop and allow herself to be caught. The deer mother told the girl the story about the girl's mother, who birthed her, dug a hole, made a bed of leaves and boggy grass, and left her. The deer mother told a story about how the deer and her fawns found the girl. The deer mother told a story about how the deer mother nursed the girl, how the fawns kept the girl warm until winter, and how the deer mother went to Nelson Ledges to gather clothing for the girl. The deer mother told a story about the uncle and his friends, about how the uncle and his friends will come to find her, how they will kill the deer mother and her fawns, and how the girl must run and then stop and allow herself to be caught so she can go back to the farm and tell the story about her mother and her deer mother and the fawns.

The next morning the uncle and his friends went into
Eagle Creek Reserve to look for the girl and the deer.
The girl's uncle and his friends found the deer in the same
valley where the uncle had spotted them the day before.
The uncle and his friends chased the deer and the girl.
One of the uncle's friends shot one fawn while another
friend shot the second fawn. One of the uncle's friends
shot the deer mother, and the uncle chased the girl. The
girl ran fast, and she ran as she was told she would by the
deer mother. And then she stopped as she was told she
would. The uncle caught her and carried her back to the
farm. All of this happened exactly as it did in the deer
mother's story. When the girl arrived at the farmhouse,
her mother was not there. She was in the fields, checking
the crops. The girl began to tell the story of her mother,
who birthed her, dug a hole, made a bed of leaves and
boggy grass, and left her. The uncle brought his sister
forth from the fields where she had been checking the
crops. The girl told her mother the story of her mother.
"It seems while you spent all your hours in the fields,
the Sun-Father had made you pregnant. Your belly grew
large. Your belly grew large as you walked in the fields for
a time. Your belly grew large, very very large. Your belly
grew large and then the ache in your belly grew large.
When the ache in your belly grew large, you walked across
the field, across the street, through the writer's property
and into Eagle Creek Reserve. You followed the creek.
You went on until you came to a bog. You sat below a
large oak tree on the edge of the bog near the creek. The
ache in your belly grew large. The ache in your belly grew
very very large. You could not see for a moment, and the
ache in your belly grew larger until I was born. When I
came out, you dug a hole. In the hole, you made a bed of
leaves and boggy grass, and you placed me in the hole,
atop the bed. You washed yourself and your clothes in the
creek, and you followed the creek back to the fields, and
the fields back to your home."

THE GIRL

The girl came to live on the farm with her mother and her uncle. The girl came to walk in the fields, checking the crops like her mother. She spent all day in the fields, plucking earworms from the feedcorn or searching the soybeans for black leaf blight. When the following spring arrived, the farmers again complained to the rangers that their fields were overrun with deer. The rangers again allowed the farmers to enter Eagle Creek Reserve for a short time to hunt the deer who were overrunning their fields. The girl could run fast, and her uncle allowed her to come with him, and allowed her to carry a rifle. The girl ran in the valley where she once ran with her deer mother and the two fawns. The girl spotted some deer. The girl fired her rifle. The writer cannot say who or what the girl shot. The writer can say, with confidence, that the girl came to Nelson Ledges to live in the ravine town with her deer ancestors. The writer can say, with confidence, that in the evenings, when the town comes alive, the girl will tell the story of the girl and the deer.

If there is no perception which is not full of memory, then this:

Outer darkness

looks like a liar inside

I learned by heart
that a fold in the brain
woven

or welded together
in the swale light
where the yeasty Ohio meets
another in fellowship

& the vegetation is ranker
but richer, like a rotting whale
whose oils survived
looking
for the word erstwhile

in outer darkness

& in easterlies

whilst flower again

while the fold in the brain

                not woven

                or welded together
                in the swale light
                where the yeasty Ohio meets
                another in fellowship

       & the vegetation is ranker
       but richer, like a rotting whale
       whose oils have survived

                looks like a liar
inside

       which himself looks
       for the word erstwhile

                  in outer
darkness

& in easterlies

As it should be, the family sold the farm.

Like a tornado who be not round around the belly, the
family moved westward.

When the rural Ohioans came to visit they felt the desert
resembled the moon.

The family thought perhaps they were meant to live on a
boat on Lake Mead.

Or, in an r.v.

The family thought they'd open a bar.

The family thought, what about gambling? What about
slot machines?

Looking back, the family liked to wonder:

Were we a colony out there in the woods?

Were we a city on the hill, a reed shaken by the wind, thorns
in our side?

Were we tempted and tried?

Were we a bicentennial learning to ride a bicycle, daddy
shouting encouragingly behind?

Were we so 19th-century to think we could build something,
open a factory?

The things the family made besides groceries:
vans, travel trailers, cabinets, electric cars, boat lifts, rental
properties & babies.

I almost forgot, for awhile, between the land and Las Vegas,
the family lived in Youngstown, Ohio.

That's where the family was born again.

A History of the Human Family

From A Far
What nationality
or what kindred and relation
what blood relation
what blood ties of blood
what ancestry
what race generation
what house clan tribe stock strain
what lineage extraction
what breed sect gender denomination caste
what stray ejection misplaced

THERESA HAK KYUNG CHA, *Dictee*

A History of the Human Family

From A Far
What nationality
or what kindred and relation
what blood relation
what blood ties of blood
what ancestry
what race generation
what house clan tribe stock strain
what lineage extraction
what breed sect gender denomination caste
what stray ejection misplaced

THERESA HAK KYUNG CHA, *Dictee*

To find our First Family
what do we peer through,
what manhole or anthole?
what foxhole or portal?
what Afar Triangle?
It was 2.5 million years ago,
& it was eternal.

1974 finds
Lucy alone
what light, light
in a gully
what diamonds in the sky
what Dinkenesh
what beautiful, what wonderful.
We find her afar
& we love her.
We send her afar
(Cleveland, Ohio)
& O.Lovejoy
we reconstruct her
what lovejoylove
what finds her

1975 finds
13 diminutive hominids
clustered together.
They met with tragedy.
Naturally, they became a family.

1992finds root
finds ground floor,
finds Ardi
&lovejoy in embrace
at Kent State
what monogamy moves
on two legs
what strength
brings me loads of fruit
loads of tubers
brings me some
six million years
afar to find you

Anyone here know how
we're all related?
Anyone here know what
what happened to what
caste of bards
charged with singing
what pedigree, what nationality, what ancestry?

Anyone here know what's better?
Polygyny or Polyandry
Virilocality or Uxorilocality
The Hindu Undivided Family (HUF)
or Living Apart Together (LAT)
more mommies or more daddies or a wolfpack of nannies?

Anyone here know the difference between
the Blent family, the Bent family, or the Avunculate family
Matrilocalities or Bilocality or Neolocality
Walking Marriages or Working from Home?

Anyone here know what's preferred
the family that prays together
or the family that stays together
to marry or to burn?

Anyone here know
how we became
closekin gathered together
or closekin outgoing
closekin closing in
on one another?

2010finds what
monogamous birds
in our trees sound like babies.

For preservation purposes,
we set up their little beds
as far from ours
as the house allows.

They wake me
&wake me eternally.

Mine Will for Mine Kind

Mine will will put you out this house
if my will wills it, it will.
Mine will will open itself to you again
will it not. It will. Fine. Sure. You hate me, fine.
Nothing you can do or say will make my will
not love you. Nothing will. Nothing
obeys me like the bee I release.
I open the door & out he will go.
Sure. Fine.
Mine father met a bear in the forest
&commanded it "go home,"
& his will made it happen.
Sure, his will be done. It will. Fine. Sure.
Mine husband will say,
"but he obeys by staying where he's found."
& verily I say unto him, Fine. Sure.
Mine will
will be done
when I die.
Fine.
Mine will
will be left
for you to find
if you will.
Sure. Fine.
My kind.

Why I Need Family

1.
mine extended infancy

2.
mine history:
food & its scarcity

3.
mine enemies

4.
mine chronic (not seasonal)
sexual excitability

5.
mine dear family
mine training agency

6.
mine most durable
most ancient dream

Look at the beautiful flower
one member says
while the other takes it to her mouth
&justlikethat
devoured

what animation
what anima
what clod
what erring
what worship
what warship
what book is this
what tender plant, root of the dry ground
what reeds & rushes
what lame man leaps as a hart
what avalanche
what footpath into astonishment

I must bear it

what fulfills her name by slipping off,
what beautiful, what gone
what name blooms in June
what name means dream, sun, pearl
what child is mine &mine child
what name, Son of Stone
what name, Field of Wood
what "yesternight when you got me up to pee"
what sleeping, dead weight
did I lay down again
what delivery
to what most bewildering dream

I must bear it

what primitive family
what military family
what spiritual family
what cyclopean family
what gorilla family
what mob family
what fisher family
what Iroquois family

what language family
what nepotism
what badblood
what bloodmoney
what servile property
what assumption of power
what brothers came together to kill
what father
what patriarchal horde formed

I must bear it

what wandervogel
what naturmensch
what white flight
what back-to-the-land
what sustainability
what ecovillage
what permaculture
what oldest relative drinks
what oldest relative doesn't
what big black woodburning stove
what tire swing
what home for hornets
what hayloft filled with holes

I must bear it

what mole or twin
what perfectly normal baby within
what open wound sends her home from school again
what's always getting in the way of this but them
what guilt
what grief caused by clinging blindly
to the vice of what family
what littermates
what nipple sustains thee

what suckled by
what herded by
what housed by
what farmhouse
what longhouse
what roundhouse
what flophouse
what −beth
what hold
what household
what House of Abraham
what parenthold
calms what out-of-control toddler
what God is where you are not
but the Father
what suicidal altruism
what mother killdeer's hurtwing
what totem come to fetch its own kin

I must bear it

1977finds
house of saud's
daughter stoned to death
&one Burchfield sister (9yrs old)
locked in a closet
while the other (13 yrs old)
aborts her father's baby

You & You are my uterine kin
thy love lights twilight
but what does it bring?
Not eternal food
Not eternal wakefulness
Not evidence
Not presence
but something just as filling,
just as draining.

A Poem for Mine Own People

what upwardly mobile
mammals came down from the trees
to what open country

what familyfamine
what landand
what totems:
the yak & the yam & the wild dandelion

what genes pass between us
what heart of my heart, apple of my eye, crooked bone of my side

what doesn't end with death
but family
bury & call upon me
ancestors-to-be

Did I Invent This Event

I remember beating the animal
inside myself
till it was bloody and looked
like I felt

I could never sincerely say
what the animal was
since it hardly resembled
itself

but a ground hog
comes to mind
or something that dug
deep
and stayed underground
until the sun shone
while we waited by its hole
for it to see
or not
its shadow
and tell us
if we'd hunker down
another month or two
below the leaves
or if we'd blow
the leaves
from the ground
and put our noses
to the bulbs
but any beaten animal
can hardly see straight
and so if it was a ground hog
he stayed under
ground perhaps putting his head down
to rest

while the rest of us stayed put
or hunkered down
or did whatever badly beaten selves do
for the rest
of the winter.

The family built a cabin in Colorado.

The family was born again.

The family did heroin.

The family was born again.

The family had children.

The family was born again.

Personal Poem Including Opium's History
for my brother

> "the whole of my past life —not as if recalled by an
> act of memory, but as if present and incarnated in the
> music; no longer painful to dwell upon, but the detail
> of its incidents removed... and its passions exalted,
> spiritualized, and sublimed..."

THOMAS DE QUINCEY, *Confessions of an English Opium-Eater*

Don't worry. I came only to tell you how beautiful the snow.
If we could bundle and bring it to our mouths, if we could bottle.
There were the Opium Wars and then the history drops off
till Vietnam.
Besides the world's first authentic antidepressant,
there are other things that are warm & tingly.
Like women, *full of caresses & deceptions* (Baudelaire).
Like limbs falling asleep.
Like lying in warm saltwater (Burroughs).
Like Summer in Ohio.

Clearly, you are considering how it grows:
"Persian White has the largest bulb and subsequently highest yield.
Poppies DO like a bit of companionship."
I learn to avoid all searches beginning with H or O.

We know it's as old as copper in Mesopotamia, but it may be older.
We know fossilized seeds, hul gil plant of joy.
We know Hypnos & Somos & what about Marcus Aurelius?
We know some Neanderthal, some Swiss Lake, some Neolithic
    poppy seed cake.
We know laudanum, thing to be praised.
We know mexican mud, china white, yellow peril.
Anchor Of Life, Milk Of Paradise, Hand Of God, Destroyer Of
    Grief

& we know what it cures: *poison and venomous bites, chronic headache, vertigo, deafness, epilepsy, apoplexy, dimness of sight, loss of voice, asthma, coughs of all kinds, spitting of blood, tightness of breath, the lilac poison, jaundice, hardness of the spleen stone, urinary complaints, fever, colic, dropsies, leprosies, the trouble to which women are subject, melancholy and all pestilences* (Galen).

colic!

                   &to think I spent last summer in the gripping
                   darknesssleeplessscreamingdepths of that
newborn illness
all the while our own mother saying,
"she must think the world is pure pain"
& were it but a century before
what we could have done for her!
what local apothecary
what tincture
what Godfrey's Cordial,
what Street's Infant's Quietness
what Atkinson's Infant Preservative
what Mrs. Winslow's Soothing Syrup
might have shushed her to sleep?

That reminds me!
You comforted me.
The photo —beautiful four-year-old boy holding baby.
Every sibling has one, don't they?
Every parent of two or more places their children on the sofa
& bribes for smiles.
You comforted me.
While I was a frightened child,
you lived your schoolboy days bravely.
You let me sleep on your floor.
You comforted me.
I'm sure it was 1983, or 1984.
Whatever the year,

some bully on the bus badgering,
Mom & Dad splitting,
a badbad boyfriend,
You comforted me.
The retreat for dysfunctional families
on the banks of the Erie.
You comforted me.
&not least of all:
my dead bunny needing burying.
That houdini animal,
that stupid animal
ate rat poison.
He deserved to die.
He was covered in flies.
Before you placed his body in the shoebox,
you hosed him off.
You comforted me, etc, etc.

& yet *a suffering of his cells alone* (Burroughs).

Better to damn this sentimentality to some forever-burning-
inferno where
    nothing changes
Or better to wrap it in a tight little bundle & hide it under the bed
Or better to bury it alongside the bunny
Or better to put it on the bus to be bullied
Or better yet to be the badbad boyfriend who doesn't show
Or better, at the very least, to beat it with a stick.
Or, instead, remember something Claudia once said:
Risk sentimentality or who will care about your damn poem?
You comforted me.

we all have natural opiates & a drive for more (Baudelaire).
it is akin to learning (Biederman).
to concern oneself with something other than life & death (Cocteau).

Here's a question:
What year did the Greek God of Dreams offer his name to
    Morphine?
Sometime after 1819.
you know them by their sleep (Sergeant Thomas/ Uncle Doug).
Perhaps it is important what happens in *my* dreams. Just recently:
Nana died. It was this year (2010). We were all there. Even Aunt
Paulette. A week had passed. You said to Dad, "you must bury
your own dead." "Yeah," he said. We went to the rental property
where her body was being kept. Some other family was living
there. The kids were using pool noodles as swords. The mother
and grandmother were making tamales. The T.V. was on. Dad
poured something over Nana's head. It fizzled. She started to
move. She opened her eyes. They were tiny like the eyes of a
rodent. I said, "I'm sorry, I love you, thank you." She smiled.
Then she disappeared.

For he on honey-dew hath fed.
For he had Helen's happy thought.
& did drop into the wine bowl
grief's ease, funeral tea. (Coleridge)
I see nothing between you & me
but our entire history.
Look.
See.
I suppose you will hate me,
but instead call me Henrietta, call me Hetty.
Instead, let's talk about your closet full of weed.
If I could say sorry for that disclosure, I would.
But that's too "the author-(to her brother)-to her book."
Too Anne Bradstreet for me.

Yo-Ho! Sweet opium and tea (Hart Crane).

A part of the history I can't get enough of:
those New Englanders, pious souls *terrified of touching* (Williams)
imported 24,000 pounds of opium in a single year.

Thomas Jefferson grew the peculiar poppy.
Benjamin Franklin, looking for relief from kidney stones,
was known to trade his first & most beloved virtue,
TEMPERANCE, for opium.
Our susceptible ladies, with light eyes
& flaxen hair, can be found in Chinatown (Dr. Wright).
& concerning civil war suffering?
I quietly took opium (Mary Chestnut).
& what's the relationship between popularity & embarrassment?
In 1898, Bayer announced its wonder drug, Heroin.
95% of it comes from Afghanistan (US State Dept).
So there you have it.
There are certainly other places to look for this history,
like the 1970's perfume industry:
Opium: The Fragrance You've Always Loved (Yves Saint Laurent).
Or the mental health community:
Get a good book on grief
& grieve the loss of all you'd hoped your son would be (Family Counselor).
I grieve that grief can teach me nothing (Emerson).
I grieve that *all pleasure is the result of relief* (Burroughs).
& there are certainly other reasons to quit writing,
like it's nobody's business,
nor is it of interest
but principally:
Resemblance.
My daughter.
Your eyes I see.
Your timeline,
not unlike my own child's,
from birth forward
intact, coherent.
But from this moment on
it blurs & then, it drops off.

High Park Fire, Colorado 2012

> Kiss of our agony Thou gatherest,
> O Hand of Fire
> gatherest—
>
> HART CRANE

Picture the house being unbuilt and then picture its build, its body
    strong, sturdy.
The door unhinged and placed back on the truck.
See the beams coming down, and then beam light through them.
It is all light now, all air.

It smells like chemical. Alchemical.
The list of what we forgot and the forest's lisp indistinguishable:
guns firing in the fire, sapphire cross crossed over,
steel mill clock ticking still.

The wolves, in their sanctuary, in their fire dens, survive.
All newly fertilized.
Likewise the mountain lions, the bears, the magpies, and the deer.
May they find in the breadth of this wood, their bread, as we had.

The Underflow

I am shown
a generosity

so muddied
at the muddy bottom

of a question I forget to ask
until it's fished out

but bloated but
in the manner of a net

a web of causal connections
attached to its corners

gently moving over
the surface of the water

how come the road
couldn't have stayed followed

by way of hollowed out
logs & paddles

made of pawpaw wood
rather than by the crows

alone to the moment
when the Monongahela

the Allegheny
the Ohio meet

I hate the underside
of an idea

but I like the underside
of grass that grows

underwater
& I've seen it from there

blossom
as if the water had suddenly

stopped
& then surged forth

from there
I can see a shoal

of tadpoles
drowning themselves

I hate the idea
of the Ohio

as a magic carpet
into the heart

of the continent
a great gift

of geography
a gleaming highway

carrying a tide
of settlement

& expansion but
I despise

the idea of the three rivers
as my family tree

their canals
tributaries & branches

meeting
& later the Mississippi

by its side
for miles

until along comes my baby
floating

in a basket
down the Colorado

I despise all such
undertows

& the fact that I've never
heard steamwhistles

or boatmen's bugles
I've never traveled

aboard *The Messenger*
The Telegraph

The Gladiator
The Ohio Belle

or *The Great Republic*
nor have I put my foot

in the Ohio
anymore than you

& the Niagara
I abhor the Niagara

in winter
the difficult beauty

of its frozen falls
and all they've

come to represent.

The Gnarly Nest Experience and Expression Make

The unorganized movement of time, smooth and predictable,
    bedevils us, covers us with a glorious varnish.
One day vanishes into another until Experience sees what we no
    longer need:
The hoed over load of unripe vegetables
burrs and thistles
beds of straw and springs
the silent thing spooling out over the edge of the property
    no one owns.

Doesn't it look like something you've seen before, whirling out of
    control?
The past is not something we have, but something we undergo.

I know from Experience a howling Ohio with hands all around
    groping.
From Experience, I know the word that stoops, sits its little
    bottom down on the ground, hisses, threatens, spits itself out.
And I know its antonym, hogging up all thought.

Experience is like a child peering through the window to see what
    light is like.
It's like light, something we know but can't quite recall in the dark.
It's like the dark, deaf, but pressed upon to hear.

When we meet it, face-to-face, we have nothing to say.
What remains but to loot our own home?

Searching the garage for a hoe,
we find something sharper and better for sowing:
we find a word that waits on the tips of our tongues to be sung.
Come forth peril, little pearl in the darkness.

FENCE BOOKS

POETRY

House of Deer	Sasha Steensen
A Book Beginning What and Ending Away	Clark Coolidge
88 Sonnets	Clark Coolidge
Mellow Actions	Brandon Downing
Percussion Grenade	Joyelle McSweeney
Coeur de Lion	Ariana Reines
June	Daniel Brenner
English Fragments A Brief History of the Soul	Martin Corless-Smith
The Sore Throat & Other Poems	Aaron Kunin
Dead Ahead	Ben Doller
My New Job	Catherine Wagner
Stranger	Laura Sims
The Method	Sasha Steensen
The Orphan & Its Relations	Elizabeth Robinson
Site Acquisition	Brian Young
Rogue Hemlocks	Carl Martin
19 Names for Our Band	Jibade-Khalil Huffman
Infamous Landscapes	Prageeta Sharma
Bad Bad	Chelsey Minnis
Snip Snip!	Tina Brown Celona
Yes, Master	Michael Earl Craig
Swallows	Martin Corless-Smith
Folding Ruler Star	Aaron Kunin
The Commandrine & Other Poems	Joyelle McSweeney
Macular Hole	Catherine Wagner
Nota	Martin Corless-Smith
Father of Noise	Anthony McCann
Can You Relax in My House	Michael Earl Craig
Miss America	Catherine Wagner

PROSE

Prayer and Parable: Stories	Paul Maliszewski
Flet: A Novel	Joyelle McSweeney
The Mandarin	Aaron Kunin

OTTOLINE PRIZE

Inter Arma	Lauren Shufran

MOTHERWELL & ALBERTA PRIZE

FENCE MODERN POETS SERIES

NATIONAL POETRY SERIES

ANTHOLOGIES & CRITICAL WORKS

LA PRESSE

CONTEMPORARY FRENCH POETRY IN TRANSLATION
EDITED BY COLE SWENSEN